MEETING EVERY CHALLENGE

The Life and Times of
Raymond Glen Robertson

MEETING EVERY CHALLENGE

The Life and Times of

Raymond Glen Robertson

As told to Edith Coffin Robertson

© Copyright 2008 Edith Coffin Robertson

ISBN: 978-0-9798633-7-0

Printed in the United States of America

Cover design by Alicia Robertson

Rp

Robertson Publishing
59 N. Santa Cruz Avenue, Suite B
Los Gatos, California 95030 USA
(888) 354-5957 · www.RobertsonPublishing.com

Introduction

One year when Ray and Edith were in Hawaii they went to visit the famous Mauna Loa volcano. They strolled through the lava beds, took pictures of the hot lava flow, the rough "aa" lava and the smooth and ropy "pahoehoe." The spatter cones and pahoehoe lava tubes were interesting. Ray leaned over a hot gas eruption, pretended to wash his hands in the yellow sulfur clouds of a fumarole as Edith snapped his picture. They got more than a snapshot memory. Ray, breathing too deeply of the sulfur, was immediately stricken with asthma.

Ray's asthma was so severe he had to stay inside in air conditioned isolation for two weeks. He read everything he could get his hands on, watched TV until the pictures blurred, then sat in desperation, bored—nothing to do.

"*Now* will you write your biography?" pleaded Edith. She had been imploring him for ages to write his memoirs so his kids and grandkids would know more about their roots. With nothing else to do and with a nagging wife ever present, Ray finally got to work and produced his biography. It was done roughly, with many asides and flashbacks. Ray wrote with difficulty as memories crowded, declared afterward that he would not rewrite or smooth out the writing.

"Bad enough to do it once," he growled. "People will sure think I'm vain." When Edith and Ray returned to California they fit a few snapshots into the story, then put it all together at the Copy Department of their store, Los Gatos Office Equipment & Supply. And there it rested for, oh—a long time.

Over the years Ray would talk, explain something, often using an illustration or two out of his past to clinch his point. "That should be in your life story!" Edith would pounce. "You really should write it over and put in those sidelights." The years passed and Edith kept nagging. Finally Ray gave in, and rewrote the whole thing but only on condition that all the relatives be told that the idea was Edith's and Edith's alone.

Hereby be ye notified:
This expanded autobiography is the result of
Ray's nagging wife, Edith, who made him do it.

Robertson

Blair Castle, Blair Atholl, was the home of the Duke of Atholl and dates from 1269. More than 30 rooms are on view and they contain an impressive collection of Jacobite relics, furniture, china, lace and armor, along with many family portraits. It is open to the public from 10 a.m. to 5 p.m. from the first Sunday in May to the second Sunday in October. ◈

Robertson

Clann Donnachaidh takes its Gaelic name from *Donnachadh Reamhar,* Duncan the Fat, who led the Clan in support of his friend and kinsman, Robert the Bruce. This Duncan claimed descent from the Celtic Earls of Atholl and was therefore known officially as *Donnachadh de Athiola.*

The historian Skene states for the Robertsons of Struan, in Perthshire, that they are the oldest Family in Scotland, and are descended from Scotland's earliest Kings.

It was a Robertson of Struan who captured the murderers of James I. As a reward, he chose to have his own lands of Struan raised to a Barony and took for his motto "Glory the Reward of Valour".

The Robertsons were intensely loyal to the House of Stewart. After the Forty-Five many were forced, for safety's sake, to take other forms of their name: Duncan, Connachie, MacConnachie, Duncanson.

Their Chief is styled Struan Robertson. BADGE—**Fine-leaved Heath, Bracken.**

Before I Was Born

Daniel Robertson was born in Scotland, June 12, 1804. He was brought to the United States as a baby at the time when Thomas Jefferson was President. The family settled in New York, later moved to the newly organized state of Illinois in Madison County, then in Morgan County. Early Galena lead miners in the those days went up the Mississippi River in steamboats in the spring, worked the lead mines, and in the fall returned. As there was a similarity between their migratory habits and those of the fish called "suckers" the Illinoisans have ever since been called "suckers."

The lead miners, traveling over the Galena trail, told the Robertsons of the fine country in Knox County, reported it to be the best through which the trail passed. Knox County (named for General Knox, a Revolutionary War hero) was about equally divided between prairie and timber, had many streams, contained much rich fertile land.

In 1828 Andrew Jackson defeated John Quincy Adams for the U.S. presidency; Washington Irving and James Fenimore Cooper were writing for America; Noah Webster's dictionary was published; the Baltimore and Ohio Railroad (B&O), America's first railroad, was inaugurated; and Daniel Robertson, his brother Alexander, and Richard Matthews (later to become brother-in-law) became the first permanent settlers in Knox County, Illinois. They came in February, 1828, with two yoke of oxen pulling their loaded "prairie schooner" wagon. They drove eighty head of hogs ahead of them.

They began the work of settling and changing a wild, uncultivated country. With their "Barshare" plow they prepared a few acres of ground and planted corn. They harvested forty bushels to the acre that first year, were able to supply their own needs, give some to their hogs, and had corn for the immigrants that soon followed. The hogs, subsisting mostly on acorns and other nuts found in the woods, in time gradually extended into a large herd.

Life was not easy. Daniel, Alexander and Richard endured the trials and hardships of a new and wild country as they began the work of settling the uncultivated county. Indians threatened, and the Indian dogs constantly raided the herds of hogs. There were no fences, each settler allowed his cattle and hogs to run at large, fixing ear marks for identification. After the hogs were grown they had to be driven to market.

One old timer told of hiring sixteen boys to help him drive 1,300 head of hogs to Fort Dearborn (later it was called Chicago), a small town, situated in the midst of miry swamps.

In 1842 the large packers gave 1 ½ cents a pound for dressed hogs, and 3 ½ cash or 4 cents in trade for green hams and lard.

Often the early settlers "tried out" (heated to melt the fat) the lard over their fire-places, a hot unpleasant job requiring round-the-clock watching. Money was little known, almost all business was done by barter. Taxes and postage, however, had to be paid by money and letters often stayed in the nearest post office for want of twenty-five cents, or two "bits." To earn two bits a man might have to work several days in his spare time. Two or three letters in a month was considered very heavy mail.

Men often traveled many miles "bee hunting." In that unsettled land they might travel for weeks without meeting another person. A good bee hunter, carefully watching the direction of flight would discover the wild bee hive. As soon as the men felled the tree they rushed to capture their booty before it was ruined by running out on the ground. Large trees sometimes yielded gallons of honey.

Daniel Robertson married a Miss Mary Maxwell November 25, 1830. Theirs was the first marriage license issued in Knox County, Illinois. They homesteaded 640 acres of rich river bottom land on which they built their log cabin and storage sheds.

No doubt their first home was typical, made of trees of uniform size, notched and chinked and daubed to prevent the wind from whistling through. A wide chimney place was made of sticks, laid in cob-house fashion and filled with clay or stone. The fireplace was large enough to hold a back log as big as the strongest man would carry. On either side were huge kettles, over all was a mantle on which they placed the tallow dip. In one corner stood the larger bed for the old folks, under this, the trundle bed for the children; in a corner stood a huge spinning wheel with a smaller one beside it; in another corner was the pine table; over the door hung the rifle and powder-horn; while around the room were scattered a few splint-bottomed chairs and three legged stools.

Early settlers were too busy to be concerned with the Indian stone axes, chisels, arrowheads or war-axes which they occasionally discovered, and it was much later that the curious Indian mounds, a very common part of the landscape, were investigated.

In time, with typical Scotch thriftiness, the Robertson family became well-to-do and started investing surplus money in Knoxville. Knoxville eventually became a suburban part of Galesburg. The increase in real estate value was unbelievable.

There was an advance in value, during the early years when settlers were pouring into the area, ranging from 300 to 1,000 percent in a five year period. The Robertson investments consisted of real estate and residential property which they rented to new residents.

My great-grandfather, John Robertson, the son of Daniel Robertson, married Belle Briggs, of English-Welsh descent. John Robertson was the sturdy old patriarch of our family. He was a Goliath of a man, stood well over six feet, weighed around 225 pounds. He had a large head with a mane of white hair and a flowing white beard. One time, while still on the farm, a bull charged him. He picked up a large piece of timber for protection and with one mighty swing he slew the bull.

Eventually the family sold the hog farm to retire in Galesburg. I was just five and Louise was only three when we first became aware of our great-grandfather. We remember him selling bagged candy from a wagon pulled by his old horse, Barney. Nearly every morning we would find a bag of candy left on the porch of our home. The old man was in his eighties then but still a sturdy Scotchman who wanted to keep busy.

When great-grandfather John Robertson was on his death-bed the relatives, Louise and I included, were all gathered around. There seemed to be a definite knock at the door, but when someone opened the door no one was there; at that very moment my great-grandfather died. Back in those days that was known to the general public as the death knock.

The next Robertson, Charles Franklin Robertson, was a typical rich man's son. He graduated from Knox College. In those days few graduated even from high school. John inherited the family fortune. He married Lura (John called her "Lurie") Martha Anderson. She was of English descent, was born near Henderson, Illinois. Her mother, Sarah E., was still active at the age of 92.

Charles Franklin Robertson (usually called Frank) was profligate, early started gambling, drinking, and driving fast horses, leading the dissolute life of the over-indulged. He sold property after property to pay his debts.

Finally, from the vast Robertson holdings there was left only one big house and side lot, 1167 Monroe Street, Galesburg, Illinois. The huge home was nicely furnished, had a beautiful organ which my grandmother played with great skill. Frank, money gambled away, later became a painter, contracted lead poisoning that made him a cripple. He spent his final years, quite tamely, in a wheelchair.

Charles and Lurie had three children. Fred Lloyd was born December 21, 1882 at Galesburg, in Henderson Township, Illinois. On Fred's birth certificate, signed by his uncle, W. D. Anderson, Fred's dad was listed as a farmer. Harry Charles Robertson was born September 15, 1884, almost two years after Fred.

Edna Robertson was born much later, around 1897. Louise remembers a picture of Edna, about eight years old, wheeling Ray in his buggy. Edna's first husband was named Wilson. They had two children, Lucille and Buddy. When the children were quite young their father was killed in a hunting accident. It was before the days of aid to the poor, Edna scrounged for employment, worked hard in a laundry. She remarried later but died shortly afterward. The end of the

Robertson Illinois holdings came when Edna's new husband inherited the big family home.

Harry must have inherited his size from old Daniel Robertson for in a few years he was taller than Fred. At school some of the rougher boys began picking on Fred and his brother. Fred, being smaller, was picked on oftener than Harry. The net result of this was that Fred became a real scrapper, so much so that he was called the champion fighter of the east part of town. Fred often came to the aid of his larger young brother. Once when they were asked, "What are you, anyway, Democrats or Republicans?" The boys answered, "Neither, we're just common people." No doubt that was enough to cause another fight.

Great Grandparents - Grandparents - Harry and Fred

Both boys were good students. Fred graduated from Galesburg High School in 1901 and took some correspondence courses in higher accounting with La Salle Extension University and with the International Accountants Society of Chicago, Illinois. Upon graduation from high school Fred and Harry went to work. Harry took a position as bookkeeper for a local store.

Fred became a delivery man with horse and wagon for Anderson & Company of Galesburg.

It was about this time that the boys became acquainted with the Lantz family. Fred Robertson left with us a copy of a June 1, 1900 census report. It says that at that time on 1457 Williams Street, Galesburg, Knox County, Illinois there lived: Carroll Lantz, head of the family, born in Sweden, immigrated in 1891 and naturalized in 1891 and Eida, wife, born in Sweden, immigrated and naturalized in 1891. Their children are listed. Alfreda was the older girl. At the time Fred became acquainted with Freda the mother was dead and Freda was doing all the housework.

Freda's family had lived near Stockholm, Sweden. They had emigrated to this country when Freda was a little girl, eight years old. Her folks had owned a fish cannery and, of all things, a horse blanket factory. They were manufacturing, in a small way.

In the Sweden of those days the people were hard working, honest, tried their best to pay their way in life, but times were hard and the townspeople learned to rely on the Lantz family in years of famine. The townspeople heard from relatives who had migrated to America how much easier life was in their new homeland. They were told eggs were as plentiful in America as potatoes were in Sweden. Grandpa Lantz sold his businesses and they were soon on a boat sailing to America, the land of plenty. My mother (Freda) told about how thrilled they were to see a large whale spouting in mid-ocean. They came to Minnesota, of course, where so many other Swedish people settled.

They were not in Minnesota long before my grandfather was offered a job as engine oiler at the C.B. & O. Railroad roundhouse. He had the reputation of being a hard worker; it was said he could do the work of two ordinary men. He had a large family but smoked a pipe, and died of cancer.

Grandmother Lantz died of tuberculosis after some ten years in America. Freda, then about eighteen took over the job of raising the family. When Freda was eight years old she had been out picking berries with her sisters on a hot summer day. She kept dropping her basket. When taken to the doctor her trouble was diagnosed as polio. Her left arm never grew beyond the size it was when she was eight years old, and it had no strength in it. She did her life work with one arm. The kids at school teased her and her parents let her drop out of school in the fourth grade. No doubt her sickly mother was only too happy to have Freda's help in the care of the growing family.

Who was to worry about the damage being done to Freda as she was to go out into the world unequipped for life's battles? No one seemed to think ahead of the misery to come for a woman with very little education, unable to hold her own in conversation, unable to manage many of the tasks out in the outside world that are easy for the educated.

Freda did not feel deprived, took hold of the family chores with ability. She learned to manage with one arm in such a skillful way that people often did not realize she had a handicap. Women wore their hair long, and Freda's was thick and heavy. She managed to put her hair up by backing her left side up against a wall, lifting her crippled left arm up to her head with her good right hand, then swiftly and neatly tucking the braids or curls up to suit her. She managed a broom with her one good arm, tucking the broom handle against her body as she swept.

Harry Lantz was musical, played piano, organ and many other instruments. The Lantz home was a center of attraction for the young people of the neighborhood. Many were the parties that were held there, Harry Lantz providing music for the singing.

Fred was very intellectual, always delving into things. He became a good hunter in the woods around Galesburg and also took up the gathering of bird eggs. I remember his collection of several hundred eggs of varied species that he cataloged neatly in a cabinet made especially for that purpose. The cabinet had a glass front with a number of drawers that were divided with one inch wood separators, both across and vertical, each little one inch square containing a bird egg of a separate species.

Fred was proficient in pen drawings in ink, drawing beautiful birds in flight, using the Spencerian writing in use at that time. He took to making personal calling cards for his friends as a hobby. Having an unusually strong and facile mind, Fred turned his attention to hypnotism, at which he became well known. With this capability he naturally became one of the entertainers at parties.

Dad related some of the remarkable things he did. At parties he would hypnotize those susceptible to his influence. Once he placed piles of salt in dishes on the table and invited his friends to eat, saying that it was ice cream. Then he snapped the crowd out of their hypnotic state. Of course that caused mixed reactions from the subjects.

One time Fred hypnotized a crowd of young people at a party and had them all down on the floor shooting dice. At this point someone shouted, "The cops!" Everyone scattered in all directions and Fred had quite a time rounding each one up and snapping them out of their trance. One young man had climbed a tree but Fred finally found him.

Another time Fred was out hunting with a friend, walking along a railroad track; the friend doubted that Fred could hypnotize him. Fred pointed to a small stream running beside the tracks and told his friend to go down and wade in it. Dripping wet, his friend came back up the tracks to the grinning Fred. "What a dirty trick that was!" he exploded.

My father would never hypnotize my sister or me. He believed that the power of one mind over the subject could have a slight weakening effect, a susceptibility to suggestion. The last time my father hypnotized anyone at a party he placed a young girl under deep hypnosis. In a hypnotic state her body became rigid and was suspended between two chairs without a center support. It was when Fred tried to snap her out of this state that he ran into trouble. She did not respond to his commands. He worked desperately over her. Slowly she came out of her comatose state. Never again, he vowed, would he ever use hypnotism.

In was while doing hypnotism that my father discovered the truth of Christ's teaching there is an unseen world of evil and good spirits around us.

At the Lantz parties Fred and Freda paired off and Harry and Elsie, Freda's sister, became interested in one another. It wasn't long until wedding bells were ringing for the two couples. A faded certificate says that Mr. Fred L. Robertson and Miss Freda L. Lantz were joined in Holy Matrimony on the 3rd day of May, in the Year of Our Lord, One Thousand Nine Hundred and Four. Elsie Lantz signed as a witness. Harry, Fred's younger brother and Elsie, Freda's younger sister, were married near the same time as my parents.

The two families often lived near each other, were close emotionally. At one time our families occupied a duplex together. I was born May 23, 1905 on 1459 North Prairie Street, in Galesburg, Illinois, in the home that Grandfather Lantz gave my mother for a wedding present. It was a beautiful two story home in a residential area. When we went back to Illinois in 1977 we visited my birth place. The house was newly painted, had a new black-top driveway. The interior was furnished in good period furniture. It was indeed interesting to behold the home where I was born over eighty years ago.

My Christian, Swedish mother
to whom I owe a spiritual and moral debt I could never repay.

Louise (3)   Ray (5)

Marriage Certificate.

STATE OF
ILLINOIS

COUNTY OF
KNOX

This Certifies, That Mr. Fred L. Robertson of Galesburg, in the State of Illinois and Miss Freda L. Lantz, of Galesburg, in the State of Illinois, were at Galesburg in said County, by me joined together in

HOLY MATRIMONY

on the 3rd day of May, in the year of our Lord One Thousand Nine Hundred and Four.

In Presence of,
Elsie Lantz.

B. L. Robinson
Police Magistrate.

Mr. Fred L. Robertson and Miss Freda L. Lantz were joined in Holy Matrimony on the 3rd day of May, in the Year of Our Lord, One Thousand Nine Hundred and Four.

Boyhood

M y Grandma Robertson made the best pies! When I was only three years old those pies used to lure me. So tempting were they that I would run away from home any chance I got, cross the railroad track to Grandma's house. Completely out of breath, I would rush into kitchen, and pant, "Grandma, pie! Grandma, pie!"

Louise was born January 13, 1907. Down through the years she was a wonderful sister in every respect.

She is always there when needed. My dad's sister Edna inherited the big three story family home and our two families lived there together for a while. After my great-grandfather John Robertson died, our great-grandmother, Belle Briggs Robertson, came to live with us on Monroe Street. We all slept upstairs except Great-grandmother.

Fred had decided to move on and his grandma was heart-broken, pleading for the young family to stay. It was little Louise's habit to go downstairs early in the morning and snuggle into bed with Grandma. One morning about

5:30 Louise toddled down to snuggle, but found her beloved grandma sprawled half out of the bed, dead of a heart attack. Louise ran to the foot of the stairs.

"Mommy, Daddy," she cried in dismay, "Grandma is asleep with her eyes open!" Everyone rushed downstairs and cried in grief, Louise hiding behind her mother's skirts, wide-eyed and fearful. It was our first encounter with death.

Glen was born to Elsie and Harry. This made a very close family as we were double cousins; for all practical purposes Louise and I had another brother. Glen was a very unusual boy. He was loved by everyone: his teachers, schoolmates, the cop on the beat - they were all his pals, one way or another. He became a Christian at an early age, for which we were thankful.

Glen Robertson, my double cousin

My father was transferred by the Galesburg office of the American Express Company to be in charge of the Quincy, Illinois, office. It was not long after this that Harry and Elsie also moved to Quincy, Harry to become bookkeeper for a hardware store on Main Street. The two families were reunited and at one particular time we occupied a duplex together.

When at Quincy our family used to go down in the evening to the banks of the Mississippi to fish. Once my mother was sitting at the edge of the river bank, fishing pole in hand, when I noticed something brown under the rock where she was sitting. Suddenly it moved. I yelled to my mother, "Move off that rock! Move fast!" As she jumped off, a large watermoccasin (called the cotton mouth in the South) slid into the water.

At Quincy, Louise and I went to good schools where a solid education in the basics was stressed. Discipline was strict, but fair. One teacher, Martha Hermans, of German descent, was a very strict disciplinarian, gave me a terrific slap one time when I stepped out of line to get a drink. But I remember those days with happiness, even to the little girl with the Buster Brown hair cut who sat opposite me in the fourth grade. I excelled in spelling and when we had the old fashioned spelling bees I would often be the very last person the be "spelled down." I hated English, couldn't see much point in the conjugation of verbs or the diagramming of sentences.

Our teachers required book reports of us. It was no chore for me as I developed a love of reading. My special joy was historical fiction. The Mohawks, David Copperfield and Captain John Smith all became a part of my life. I did not neglect the more factual reading, either. One Christmas Dad and Mother got us a twenty volume set of Books of Knowledge. I went through the entire set from A to Z!

Once I wandered down to the Mississippi River, watched with great interest as a fisherman got his boat and equipment ready to go out with his trout line. He had fifty to seventy-five hooks strung along the line and a buoy at the end. He looked up at me, invited, "Wanna come along, kid?" I accepted eagerly. We rowed out against the current and the fisherman let out his line. The boat rocked, the old fish smells were terrible, and I huddled miserably in the boat, clutching my upset stomach. As soon as we got to the end of the line the fisherman reversed direction, started for shore, pulling up on the line as he went, unhooking fish after fish. The boat rocked in the current, the smelly fish squirmed in the bottom of the boat and I got greener and greener by the minute. I was so happy to be on shore again when that fishing trip was over!

At the Webster School in Quincy we had a lot of good athletic equipment. We particularly liked "riding the waves" on the tall pole equipment from which hung twelve long chains with rope handles. Eight boys would play at once, each boy holding on to the big rope knot at the end of a chain. As soon as we were positioned one boy would get his chain around all the others. We would all run around the pole in one direction, the boy whose chain was on top riding higher and higher as we got up speed. He could be almost level with the top of the tall pole. One time I was the outside kid riding the waves when I lost my grip. I flew off into the air, landed on my stomach and face. I was in bad shape. No wonder that kind of school ground equipment is no longer in use.

It was in Quincy that the most important event of my life occurred. An evangelist named Charles Scoville came to town with the usual evangelist tent and started a series of revival meetings. The tent was huge, holding some 10,000, people. Wooden benches faced the speaker's platform and tons of sawdust covered the tent floor.

The meetings were held for thirty days. Reverend Scoville was a famous and gifted preacher. The tent was always packed and our family attended the services every night. After one particularly fine sermon on the necessity of becoming a Christian and that it was up to the individual to choose his own fate, either heaven or hell, I "took the sawdust trail". I literally ran down the closest aisle for conversion to Christianity. I have never had cause to regret my decision. It is as valid today as it was seventy-one years ago. We are all just a heartbeat away from standing before God — regardless of any or all circumstances surrounding our lives.

It was about this time that I acquired a love for books. One year I read several hundred books, but as a result I developed eye trouble and headaches over the eyes. The optician to whom my mother sent me said that I would have to give up reading so much or wear glasses. Naturally, I choose glasses, and have had to wear them all my life.

I loved the outdoors. Quincy, Illinois, had the most beautiful parks in the nation. Quincy was situated on the banks of the Mississippi River with its colorful sidewheeler steam boats. These excursion boats always carried a band for dancing and the evening excursions up the river to Keokuk, Iowa, were a regular occurrence. Our family took these excursions frequently. Down town, right in the center of town, we had a block square park complete with bandstand.

My dad was transferred again, this time to Keokuk, Iowa. Louise and I were part of a gang. There were many local gangs: Twelfth Street Gang, Thirteenth Street Gang, etc. We had wars in the schools, the blacks against the whites. The boys carried long bladed pocket knives, called "toad stabbers." It often took the police to quell the racial outbreaks. I was friends with everyone, blacks and whites, and once it paid off in a big way for me. At one fight in my school at Keokuk, a Negro boy, "Big John," who was my friend, told me to back up against the brick wall of the school. He then moved a few paces outward, flicked out his toad stabber and made himself my protector.

Once more we moved. My dad went to Austin, Texas, looking for work. There being no unemployment insurance, aid for the indigent, social security or railroad pension, Dad was strictly on his own. He walked the streets looking for work. Dad was a little man, not too strong, found it hard to make a good impression. Our situation became desperate.

Finally, one day, we were down to one dollar, Dad said to Louise and me, "Come on, kids, you're going with me this time." With one of us on either side he started out canvassing. It was as close to begging as I ever hope to come, but how brave of my Dad. He inquired at several places then at the Austin Telephone Company he was offered a job as collector.

My cousin Glen died at the age of twelve in 1920 during the world wide flu epidemic which claimed over twenty million lives before it was over. We lived in El Paso, Texas when we got the news. Aunt Agnes wrote of her shock as she was going to visit her sister Elsie, getting off the streetcar and seeing a black funeral wreath on the front door. I remember, after the letter from Aunt Agnes, in my deep misery, going out on a hill in El Paso, thinking of Glen and all he meant to me. I stood there, crying, choked with grief. It was the last time I ever cried. We made a pilgrimage back to see his grave in Quincy, Illinois in 1977, the same trip that took in my birthplace, the Webster School I attended in Quincy and all those beautiful parks in Quincy where I had roamed as a boy with my pals.

In El Paso, Texas, when I was about fourteen I belonged to a gang of neighborhood kids. We had great ways of having fun. After school we would often gather at my home, meet up in the third story cupola. Here we had a terrific time playing a card game based on action in the Chicago stock market. We got very noisy as our play went on hour after hour. "I'll bid forty for corn!" One would yell, while another screamed louder, "Sixty on wheat!" It's a good thing we were way up on the third floor.

On a windy day we would forget the Pit game, put on our roller skates and head down hilly El Paso streets. Each boy had his own home-made kite, as high as the boy was tall and as wide as the boy's wide-spread arms. Our kites were made on a wooden frame with canvas instead of paper. With the kite positioned behind our backs we held on to the cross braces with out-stretched arms. As we positioned the kites to pick up the wind, we went sailing down the street at a tremendous speed. This stunt would be impossible now with modern traffic. So... there is something to be said in favor of "... the good old days... "

Still, even though there were few cars on the streets, there were accidents. Once I was standing on the sidewalk when a car struck a boy riding a bicycle, seriously injuring the boy. I stood helpless, watched the ambulance take the boy away. An attendant, seeing me, said, "Here, son, take care of the kid's bike for him." As I stepped forward to take the bike home I noticed teeth on the cobblestones.

Saturday nights the Quincy parks would be filled with people listening to the concerts. This helped to develop a love of music within me that was to show up in following years.

My father, afflicted with asthma from birth, was told to go to Boulder, Colorado, for his health. Dad took a leave of absence of one month and we went to Boulder. Not noticing any real difference in his health we returned to Quincy. Months later he took another leave to go to Austin, Texas, thinking that the drier climate might help him but the result was the same. However by this time he had a taste of the western country and the sense of freedom that went with it. He asked for a transfer to Albuquerque, New Mexico, as night depot agent for the railroad.

A recession occurred at that time and he was bumped off the job by another railroad man with higher seniority in the district.

He then went to work for the U. S. Government in Ysleta, New Mexico, as a Government representative for the Pueblo reservation. Ysleta is located thirteen miles from Albuquerque. We had a large adobe ranch house furnished us, stables for our government team of horse: Colonel, a large black, and Charley, a large white horse. We also had a granary for the storage of hay. Dad was allotted two Indian policeman to help in times of trouble on the reservation. Dad's position was to represent the government in its dealings with the Indians on the reservation. The Indians were represented by Pablo Abeta. Abeta was a lawyer and later a judge of the local court.

Of the two ranch horses furnished us, Colonel was much the smarter. One day he used his lips to open the door to our granary where we kept the hay and grain for them. We caught him in time before he had eaten too much. Surgery often has to be performed when horses over-eat. Horses will eat oats or hay until their stomachs burst.

I used to go out rabbit hunting with a friend, a young teenage Indian. He would ride Charley and I would take Colonel. Usually, the horses were used to pull a wagon into Albuquerque for supplies so they were accustomed to being together most of the time. On one hunting trip the Indian boy got off Charley to pick up something, and casually threw the reins over the horse's head so Charley would stand. The result was a disaster.

Charley took off for the ranch house at a gallop. My Indian friend and I rode double until we got back to the ranch. There was Charley waiting for us. The first thing the horses did was nuzzle each other. Charley had lost the saddle blanket in his mad dash to get back home to the ranch, and his saddle was down under his belly.

One time our family was going into Albuquerque for supplies when the Indian policeman driving the team said, "Just a minute, I have something to do." He stood up in the wagon and took his long whip, popped it at a rattlesnake that was coiled up by the side of the road and cut the snake's head off. It was an all day trip to go in for supplies even though the distance was only 26 miles, round trip.

On the Indian Reservation there was a large round ceremonial house called a "Kiva". This was where they held their religious ceremonies and no white man was ever admitted. We could hear their chants which to us were very repetitious, "Ho, ya, Ho ya, a Ho, a Ho, a Ya, Ya." They repeated this phrase over and over in their singing.

The Indians loved sports; favorites were horse racing and a sport they called a chicken pull. After burying a live chicken in a hole dug in the sandy soil they would trot back a hundred yards and then come racing down the track, riding bare back, and try to lean over and pull the chicken out of the hole. More often than not all they got was the head. To us it seemed a cruel sport.

When I was ten or eleven years old, I became acquainted with the husband of a school teacher on the reservation, a Mr. P. S. Everybody called him by that name because his real name was long, French, and hard for us to pronounce. One day my friend Mr. P.S. came over to the ranch house and asked if I would like to go with him to hunt for an old gold mine that the Spanish Conquistadores had worked for many years. It was located in the Manzano Mountains about thirty miles from the ranch and up a large canyon called Comanche, so named because Comanche Indians had massacred a band of early settlers there.

I was excited about making the two week trip with him, so with Dad's permission, we started outfitting. It meant a couple of burros, two diamond hitch wooden racks to place on the donkeys' backs for our provisions and tent. I learned how to throw a diamond hitch over the packed animals and how to unload at night.

The first night took us about twenty miles over the desert and toward the canyon. We camped the first night at a large water hole some thirty feet across. On arrival we were greeted by a chorus of bull-frog croaks. They were really big frogs and we were lucky to shoot about thirty-five of them. We cut off their legs and peeled back the skin to the feet, cut off the feet, washed them, popped them into a frying pan along with a rabbit we had shot on our way across the desert. That night out in the desert we had a gourmet dinner.

The next morning we were up bright and early and made it to the base of the canyon just in time to have breakfast with some ranchers who lived there. It was some breakfast: hot cakes, steak, potatoes, home-made bread and lots of coffee. Ranch hospitality just can't be beat!

Across the saddle, back of the canyon, at the very top there existed a little village called Tahickee. The oldest people there told stories about their ancestors carrying out sacks of gold ore from a mine. The mine was called "La Mina de Juan Soldada" (the mine of John the Soldier). Government rangers coming up and down the canyon would stop by our camp and visit with us, giving us the latest outside news. We found gold float, which had been washed down from somewhere above us on the mountain but we never did find the source of the float. The mine opening had been closed by landslides during rain storms and underbrush too thick to penetrate. It was indeed a golden experience for me, living the rugged life of a hard rock (quartzite) gold miner.

Dad in the meantime had been in touch with the railroads and as that was predominately his field it was not long until Superintendent L.P. Bergman requested that he report to El Paso, Texas, to the main office where he began trouble shooting for the railroad.

The year was 1917 and it was here that I started high school. Fort Bliss, a large army post, is located some few miles outside El Paso and near the Southern Pacific Railroad. A local man in El Paso was hiring high school boys to sell candy and peanuts to the soldiers at the Fort. We worked on straight commission and had to catch a ride on the freight trains going by the Fort to get there. One time there was an ugly brakeman on the freight train we were hitching a ride on and he kicked us off. One of the boys was shoved off where there was a steep embankment some hundred yards down hill from the tracks. He was a sorry sight as he went down, head over heels, candy from his candy basket flying all around him.

The soldiers were housed in large square tents with twenty men to a tent. Around the edges of the tent their folding sleeping cots were end to end. Clothing, bedding, and personal belongings were stored under the cots. I was scared stiff the first time I tried to sell any candy. Luck was with me, however, as a soldier who had been drinking took me in tow and asked, "What have you got there, kid?"

"Candy and salted peanuts," came out from somewhere in me, just audible enough for him to hear.

"Come on, kid, let's do some business," he said. The first soldier we went to said he didn't have any money. "Give him a couple of bags, kid! I'll pay you for them." Every soldier in the tent got candy or peanuts, and if they couldn't pay, my drunken soldier friend paid for them. We made the rounds. I went out of that tent walking on pure air!

After a few trips selling for the man, I had thoughts of bigger profits. Why couldn't mother produce home made chocolate fudge for me—really good candy? I could buy salted peanuts at the ten cent store, rebag them (one bag into two) and make fifty percent profit for my efforts. Mother agreed and became my partner in the candy business.

My father was moved again by the railroad to Douglas, Arizona, and after a short while was sent to Hayden, Arizona, as cashier. Hayden is a copper milling town in southern Arizona. It seemed weird in 1977, to revisit the old grammar school I had attended some seventy-one years ago. The town had changed vastly since we were there, though many of the old landmarks were still around.

HAYDEN, ARIZ.

We were fortunate that we stayed some four years in Hayden before the next move. Hayden was an ideal spot for a boy to grow up. The climate was hot in summer but moderate the rest of the year. It was here that I became a second-class Boy Scout. Our Scoutmaster was the pastor of the local Methodist Church I attended. As a Scout I took many trips into the surrounding mountains which we enjoyed immensely. I remember one great two week camping trip.

We took along five gallons of syrup in our supplies for our hot cakes. It was gone the first week! Fifteen healthy boys helping themselves until the pan cakes were swimming in syrup seemed to do the trick. We captured snakes, tarantulas, and other wild life which we placed in bottles, one of our boys being a born naturalist.

The weather was so hot that we all got prickly heat. In order to get water that was drinkable we boiled water from a near-by spring. In a neighboring ranch we discovered a field of watermelons ready for harvest and of course we had to "borrow" a few. The farmer had so many!

One trip to the top of the range of mountains surrounding Hayden remains as a horrible memory. We boys all carried sling shots made out of a pair of leather throngs which were about three feet long. A leather pad with a hole cut in its center was fastened to two ends of the throngs. We felt it was a good weapon to carry as a protection against Mexican boys who also had their own sling shots. One would place a rock in the center of the leather pad, then hurl it around the head a few times before letting go of one throng. We would knot these throngs and carry them hanging from our necks. We were proud of our potent weapons.

We climbed the cliffs of the mountains surrounding Hayden. We enjoyed the majestic view when we finally reached the top of the third tier of mountains but we were too full of life to stand and admire scenery. We started rolling large boulders down the steep cliff face, watching as the rocks bounced.

Scout Alexander leaned forward to push a boulder over the cliff. His sling shot around his neck caught on a projection on the rock he was pushing. As the boulder went over it pulled Alex with it and we watched with horror as his body fell hundreds of feet to the next large mountain shelf. It took a party of men from the copper mill to traverse the rugged terrain to bring Alex's body in. It was a sorry Scout troop that wended its way back to Hayden.

We were not wealthy people, Dad drew an ordinary salary, so my mother was most frugal in clothing us. I can remember one blue serge suit that I wore for three years straight-dirt and dust was just embedded in it. I have NEVER worn a blue serge suit since!

Many Mexicans worked in the copper mill, so many that they had their own village across a tailing bed of sand from Hayden proper. Tailings were the slurry left over after the copper ore had been extracted.

I remember once when the Mexican baseball team came over to our clubhouse and challenged us to a ball game. A fight broke out after the game and we chased the Mexican kids back to their village, down our side of the canyon and across the tailing bed that separated the two towns. There, Mexican boys went for their sling shots and war was on. We got out our slings and fought back. They had the advantage of throwing down hill. A good sized rock coming out of a sling shot was a deadly thing. Those stones would hit with a resounding thud!

Those rocks coming down on us could have killed any-one of us who happened to be hit in a vital spot. The Biblical story of David killing the giant Goliath with a rock from his sling shot was no myth. No one was hurt in our war, how-ever, and we eventually broke off the fight and headed back to our clubhouse.

One year the local school board decided we would have school on New Years Day. We eighth graders took exception to what we had always considered a holiday. We made care-ful plans. We reported to school as usual. Then the girls went back home without attending class. We boys, not so tame, decided to cross the tailing beds between Hayden and the

Gila river. A wooden flume carried the tailing slurry down from the mill to the tailing beds. The tailing beds were about a mile in width and extended for miles in length.

As we reached the Gila River we found that it was in flood stage due to the snow runoff from the mountains. We hesitated at the cold rolling water. Looking back across the tailing beds we had just crossed, we saw our local sheriff on his big white horse, galloping over the beds to round us up. Our minds were made up for us by the sight of the sheriff.

The flood waters were a dirty brown with floating uprooted trees and other debris carried along with it. However, the big boys plunged in and swam the river. I was smaller and not as strong, so I took my shoes off and swam the river with one arm holding my shoes above my head. Due to the swiftness of the current we all landed about a half mile down the river on the opposite shore. We built a bonfire, dried out our clothes, then headed up the river where there was a bridge we could cross to get back home.

The next morning our punishment was handed out to us. We were forced to go to the school library after school and just sit there, no conversation, for an hour. To a boy twelve years old one full week of just sitting was real punishment. In addition we got an F in deportment on our report cards for that month.

When the water was clear we boys used to go fishing up the canyon. We also set traps under the water along the shore for raccoons. We would bait them with a shiny piece of tin can, but we were never successful in catching a raccoon. We did do well with the fishing, however.

One time after a flood when the river returned to its banks, many catfish were left stranded in pools along its banks. Our gang scooped up handfuls of the small fish and returned them to the river. When we quit our rescue work some hours lager our hands were badly cut by the sharp splines behind the heads of the wiggly catfish.

During World War I our school had a Victory Garden of several acres down along the river bottom. We grew a huge amount of vegetables there for the war effort.

About this time ambition reared its ugly head again and I thought up a new way to make money. Hayden was a dusty, sandy mill town and few housewives in town owned vacuum cleaners. I took my mother's vacuum cleaner and went canvassing up and down the hills of Hayden, offering my services in cleaning rugs, charging seventy-five cents per rug. It was hot dirty work lugging that heavy vacuum cleaner up and down those hills but it was financially profitable.

The war ended and our town had a victory parade. My sister Louise won first place in our local beauty contest. Dressed in a red white and blue gown with a Victory Crown on her head, Louise rode in the first float. After the parade was over she was given an airplane ride over the town. She was the first one of our family to ride in a plane. It was many years later that I took my first trip by air.

Louise worked in the First National Bank there as a teller and bookkeeper and was on her way to becoming a very efficient office worker.

In Hayden I had two real pals, Lynn Whitman and Ted Tweed. Because Ted and I were of small build we decided to take up boxing to protect ourselves from being picked on. The local school had a boxing instructor and we learned to use the gloves. My dad had helped me set up a boxing ring in the attic.

It had gone the gossip rounds that Ray Robertson had fixed up a boxing ring in his home—ropes, pad, and all. With my boxing training I had little trouble defending myself. One time one of the larger boys in school, Gail Wilcox, said he would like to box with me. We fixed up a boxing party at my house with Gail and me as principals. Gail outweighed me by some forty pounds and was a head taller but he knew nothing of the art of self defense. We squared off, then he came at me with a rush. I just side stepped him and threw a straight right that caught him flush in the face. It knocked him flat on his back and that was the end of the fight. With that episode I had no more challengers.

Ray Robertson's Report Card.

Ray received an F in Behavior for leaving school with friends and swimming across the Gila River after the Sheriff spotted them and rode after them on his horse.

My Bachelor Years

Dad was bumped off his position in Hayden and we moved to Flagstaff, Arizona. This was during the depression of 1921. I was only sixteen years old but I had to quit school to help earn a living for the family. Dad and I went to work for the Flagstaff Lumber Company, he in the box factory and I in the planer mill as an assistant sticker man. A sticker man is one who cuts steel plates according to a pattern book using a lathe and pattern outline. Two steel blades are made of each molding pattern then the blocks are locked onto the planer blocks. The wood is fed into the planer rollers in the front of the planer. The pattern plates cut the molding in the shape of the pattern. The planer's weight I estimate at 5,000 pounds. We had planers as large as 50,000 pounds that planed the 18 foot 2 inch planks into finished lumber. All planers were run by large leather belts some seventy-five feet long that were fitted to the long center shaft wheels at the top of the mill. The shaft was of steel and some six inches thick. It ran the length of the planer mill and on into the power house where the huge generators turned the shaft.

One day with the mill running full blast, the huge center shaft crystallized as we were feeding raw lumber into the planers. The broken shaft started shaking the mill apart. The workers rushed to get out before catastrophe hit. The foreman ran to the center of the mill and pulled the control cord. As the alarm blasts split the air the mills gradually stopped shaking themselves to pieces.

I worked at the sticker mill ten hour a day, seven in the morning till six at night for the princely sum of seventeen cents per hour or $1.75 per day. We bought our groceries at the company store at a 10% premium over other store prices in town. We are reminded of the old time song,

Saint Peter don't you call me; 'cause I can't go
I owe my soul to the company store.

Dad was next recalled by the railroad to Clarkdale, Arizona, where I continued high school. It was here that I took up the saxophone. I took private lessons from a high school teacher for about six months. I was later to own a "C" tenor and an "E" flat alto saxophone. They both saw much service, as I played in a dance orchestra in Gallup and in various surrounding towns.

Ray, budding musician

Ray   Louise

For one engagement in Breece we arrived to find no piano. That was difficult. Another time at a coal mining town two fellows started to fight and wrecked the evening for everyone. I got the fellows together to leave. The two fighters, friends again, came to beg us to stay but we walked out.

After a year and a half at Clarkdale Dad was recalled by the Santa Fe Railroad at Gallup, New Mexico, as depot agent. Louise went to work for the First National Bank. Louise was the only girl in the bank, much favored by all. Every day after the bank closed the head cashier, a young man, would go out and buy a box of candy, then he and Louise would settle in, eating candy and balancing the books.

I went to work installing a Dodge Brothers Accounting System under the direction of a Mr. A.S. Graham, a Public Accountant. I was bookkeeper and parts man for the Dodge Brothers Agency in Gallup, the Watson Motor Company. It was here that I really learned fine accounting. We turned out a four page report each month for Mr. Watson that was a gem of business knowledge. Parts of that system are still in use today by my wife and me as I make up the statements for the Los Gatos Office Equipment and Supply Co. Inc.

Again my father was sent to Thoreau, New Mexico, as depot agent, so I resigned my job and went to work for the Thoreau Mercantile Company of Thoreau, located right on top of the Continental Divide, just thirty miles from Gallup. It was on the main line of the Santa Fe Railroad which crossed the Navajo Indian Reservation. Thoreau Mercantile had the local post office and also three star routes that handled all the mail for Clauson, Crown Point and Breece, New Mexico. I handled the post office, including the mail bags for the star routes. I also waited on trade in the trading store. We bought and sold wool and bought Indian blankets, rugs, pillow tops and rugs made the Navajos. The store handled general merchandise, sold everything one could imagine. We had saddles, bridles and bits, saddle blankets, turquoise jewelry crafted by the Navajos, a complete line of groceries and farm needs.

An employee named Brownie and Mr. Jones both spoke Navajo and it wasn't long until I picked up quite a bit of the language. I found my high school Spanish came in handy because the Navajos had mixed some Spanish in their speech.

One day Brownie behind the counter, was kidding a tall Navajo. The Indian took exception to the teasing and aimed a mighty swing at Brownie. I came around the counter to help Brownie but the Indian was too fast for me and caught me with an uppercut, right on the point of the chin. (I could not eat lunch that day.) The Navajo then ran for the door but Brownie stayed behind the counter. I yelled at Brownie, "Throw a pop bottle at him!" Brownie explained later he was afraid of missing the Indian and breaking a large front window.

Dad took a month's vacation to go to Oakland and realized then that California was a beautiful place to live. The family moved to Oakland and I secured a job through a friend of mine, paying off financial paper at the Home Office of the Bank of Italy—later known as Bank of America. My work carried me from the top of the building to the basement with an auditor following me checking the payoffs. Sometimes the sums were very large, going to hundreds of thousands of dollars on different kinds of documents. Once I had to go by streetcar to the Federal Reserve with a check for seven million dollars. I looked at the check and thought, "Oh, boy! Couldn't I have fun with this!" I realized, of course, that I couldn't cash it, but it was nice to dream. The pay was lousy, $75.00 per month for my position. Banks have always been notorious for poor pay.

In a couple of weeks an old buddy of mine in Gallup, New Mexico, wired me to come back and keep his books for him for $110.00 per month for two hours work a day. I immediately accepted. Once there I picked up other accounts that paid good fees for my services.

I soon had the auditing for the Ford Dealer, Carrington Motor Company; the Drake Hotel; Bedow Brothers, Buick Dealers; Rollie Undertaking Company with a branch at Holbrook, Arizona; Gallup Independent Newspaper; and the largest company of all was the W. N. Bickel & Company, with a wholesale warehouse in Gallup and with four branch retail Indian Trading Stores on the Navajo Indian Reservation in Arizona.

I made the trip out to Bickel's Navajo Indian retail stores about every two weeks and stayed a couple of days, living at the home of Louie Sabin, the other partner in the business. Theirs was one of the most beautiful partnerships I ever handled. Strict honesty prevailed in word and operation of the business.

One day, when I was working behind the postal window, Louie Sabin's little girl came into the store. He gave her a hug and a kiss and they chatted for a while. When she asked for a candy bar he let her pick out her favorite, then walked behind the counter, drew the big company ledger out, flipped open the pages and registered the date, and wrote: Charge to L. Sabin--1 candy bar, 5 cents.

They were immensely profitable. I also did court audits for the municipal court. Those audits I received through my contacts with the funeral parlor on estates and trusteeships. One case lasted some months before settlement—an inheritance case for three little girls.

My experiences with the funeral business was interesting. Once, when taking inventory of caskets and suits of clothes in the basement, I opened an expensive copper casket leaning against the wall and discovered the body of a coal miner who had died without leaving a will. With no one to watch expenses the funeral director, appointed as administrator, proceeded to eat up the man's estate with the most costly funeral imaginable. "He left no relatives and no will," explained the director. "I may as well have the money as the next fellow—or the state."

Once I saw on the embalming table a young logger's body, in perfect physical condition, a beautiful specimen of manhood. I was told that a tree he'd had been cutting had fallen the wrong way.

One of my reasons for success in Gallup as a public accountant was that I was secretary of the local De Molay Lodge which was sponsored by the Knights Templar of the Masonic Order. I was also financial secretary of the local Methodist Church and played in the church orchestra. I was also a member of an eight-piece dance orchestra that played for the local dances. My contacts brought many accounts.

Dad decided to move back to Detroit for the railroad. In due time I became lonesome and decided to follow the family.

I sold my accounting business to a man I had working for me. He lost the business in three months. "I just don't have what it takes to handle all that work!" was the explanation I got.

I could have retired long ago if I had stayed in Gallup with that beautiful business I had going. I had a girl friend, Ethel, who wanted to get married and come east with me but I was not ready for marriage. Three months after I left Gallup she married someone else. Just wanted to get away from her parents, I guess.

In Detroit I went to work for PriceWaterhouse & Company, the premier accounting firm in the world. Their offices are all over the world with headquarters located in London. They require an accounting examination before taking anyone on their staff. After the busy income tax season was over I went to work for the accounting department of the factory branch of Willys Overland in Detroit.

I left then to become Office Manager for the Pontiac Division of General Motors in Detroit. We had the largest service department in the United States. We employed forty mechanics, occupied a six story building in Detroit.

OUR SUNSHINE BISCUIT CREW IN SOUTH BEND INDIANA

Ray - in straw hat

A year after that I went to work for Loose-Wiles Biscuit Company (now Sunshine Biscuits) in charge of their office in South Bend, Indiana. Here we had ten trucks on the road (wholesale to retail stores) and fourteen salesmen. I ordered two freight car loads of cookies and crackers per week. We were located on a spur track of the railroad with our warehouse. From there I made an audit of their branch office in Peoria, Illinois. Loose-Wiles then sent me to Detroit to be Credit Manager and Assistant Office Manager.

I had ten people under me in the office and fifty salesmen accountable to me for credits. We covered all of Michigan and parts of Illinois and Ohio with our deliveries. Loose-Wiles had some fifteen factories spread over the eastern part of the United States. We were second in size to National Biscuit Company, the largest wholesale baking company in the world.

Louise and I continued to be very close to one another over the years, sometimes sharing an apartment, sometimes going out together when no other date was handy.

Louise (24) and Ray (26)

My folks next moved to Los Angeles and I resigned my position with Loose-Wiles to join my family. Mr. B. Steinhof, manager of Chicago Bakery, called me into Chicago and asked if I would not reconsider my decision. He stated that they had planned bigger thing for me in the future. However, I explained that I was after varied experience and did not want to tie myself down to a single concern. I was very self-assured in those days. I made the move to Los Angeles with Bud, a PriceWaterhouse man.

On coming across the country we had an accident in Texas that upset us (literally). We were passing a football stadium built near the highway when a large Buick hit us from the rear. Our Ford was overturned on the driver's side, spun around for some distance and finally came to a stop. A crowd emptied out of the stadium and lifted the car back on its wheels. The car which hit us had landed in the ditch and was undamaged. The driver told us that he would meet us in the town that was looming up ahead. We were so rattled by the experience that when I told Bud to get the man's license number Bud failed to do so. The stranger, of course, did not stop in the next town but kept going across the Texas plains. The damage to our car was $150.00, almost a month's salary at that time.

After we got to San Diego we drove across the border where Bud did a little gambling. I was too Scotch to risk my money. He won a little, then we headed for Los Angeles.

Heavy fog blanketed the coast highway as we headed north. About half way up the coast we were stopped by a bunch of fellows in dress clothes who were going to play for a dance. They asked us where they were and we couldn't say except they were on the coast highway headed north. The fog was so thick that I was out on the running board trying to tell Bud where the edge of the highway was. Back in those days a running board was a necessary part of a car. An hour later a car pulled up beside us and the driver started asking directions. We all started laughing. It was the same bunch of fellows going to play for that dance! We pulled into Los Angeles the next morning. It took us all night to go 135 miles. On reaching Los Angeles we both went to work for PriceWaterhouse.

It was October 1929, I was twenty-four and the big depression had just hit. Bud and I, along with twenty-three other auditors, were sent over to audit the brokerage firm of Tucker, Hunter and Dulin, a large stock and bond brokerage firm in Los Angeles with branches in principal cities across the country.

With a stock market crash the situation was hectic. When auditing a stock and bond brokerage company the biggest part of the audit covers two main things:

1. *The cash position the firm audited (moneywise?)*
2. *Is the stock positioned in safekeeping or in transit, or in someone's account? What position is each customer in relationship to his stock; is the stock in the firm's vault, or has it been sold?*

Each stock and customers' account was reconciled on separate three by five cards with the name of the stock at the top of the card. These were made up from the customers' accounts, buying and selling records, in-transit records and stocks and bonds in the vaults. Of the twenty-five auditors originally sent to the job, Bud and I were the last to leave.

The market during the eight weeks we were there was in a state of utter chaos. There were some stock and bonds and customer accounts that we never could reconcile. In Beverly Hills people had bought heavily on a 15% margin to hold a stock. When the stock dropped they did not have the money to cover with the stock brokerage house and they were wiped out, money-wise and stock-wise. All over Los Angeles people were committing suicide.

After the Dulin audit I worked on audits on a bond house in Pasadena where falsifying the books had been going on, then an ink manufacturing firm, then to Macy's Department Store for verification of inventories.

An actors' agency in Beverly Hills was next. It bespoke money and was monied, even though there was a huge depression on. The agency was housed in what had been a bank building, very imposing from the outside. Inside, the marble floors were covered with large polar bear skins for rugs, appropriately placed. It was pure luxury as a business house.

An actor's agency is an easy audit to make. Only two of us were on this one. A good agency could make or break an actor or actress. We checked the charges to the actor's account for the commission (usually 10% of his weekly contract pay) and the period covered.

After the actor's agency I was placed on motion picture studio work exclusively, starting with First National Studios in Burbank, California. My first day I moved around the different parts of the studio and become acquainted with the routine of the work, no actual auditing being done.

My second day at First National Studios I lined up my schedule and working papers for that part of the audit to which I was assigned and began making an assessment of the accounting situation as of that date.

Studio auditing was rather interesting. I had free access to the many sets on the various sound stages. I remember one set on which Walter Pigeon was having a sword duel (in the period of around 1550.) It was extremely hot under the Kleig spotlights and the actors were in distress. With some twenty spotlights of varying sizes and intensity thrown on the scene the heat was terrible. The chief cameraman often got some relief with his boom swinging around above the set and shooting from there. The floor cameramen suffered along with the others in the heat from the lights. I finished the First National Studio and was then sent to Paramount Studios.

Some weeks were spent on that audit. There were three large studios, Paramount, Metro Goldwyn Mayer and Warner

Brothers. Paramount, the largest, faced Melrose Avenue, and covered some 24 acres in the heart of Hollywood. One hundred and thirty-five buildings and stages covered the lot. They had a separate fire department, a restaurant, a barber shop, and a separate water department. The fan mail building was in the charge of a Miss Zukor, a relative of Adolph Zukor, the President of Paramount. Scripts were made up by the dozen for each picture and I read quite a few of the scripts as I had studied scenario writing at night for some two years while in the midwest and wanted to break into the scenario department. The answer to that one is that you have to write a best seller first before you even get a chance on the inside. My pull with the relative of the President did not mean a thing.

PARAMOUNT   ADMINISTRATION   BUILDING

Paramount was very modern, being highly mechanized. All studio forms were recorded by the key punch operator. Her cards carrying information regarding every part of the studio were then sent to the "Powers Room."

The Powers Room contained the huge Power Machines that weighed tons. They were predecessors of our present large computers. The finished product, printed sheet, covered every operation of the studio. These sheets went to the accounting department consisting of some thirty accountants and bookkeepers. The results of the sheets were then tabulated on control sheets on Burroughs bookkeeping machines. From there the sheets were given to the head accountant, a woman who had been with Cecil B. DeMille ever since Paramount first started with the silent picture, "The Squaw Man".

After we completed the audit I was offered a position at Paramount being put in charge of the records covering the lot expenses and also covering the special productions of the pictures in process. At that time, before a major feature production was shot, a pilot film was made. Production costs then started accumulating on the picture. Expenses for salaries for actors, cameramen, and writers, along with the studio overhead, were started, sometimes weeks before the shooting began on the actual production. I became acquainted in a superficial way with many famous people and my two years spent with Paramount was an interesting period.

Sometimes when out on the lot in connection with overhead charges I ran into interesting sights of pictures being made on outdoor sets. Once I recall the "Sign of the Cross" being shot by Cecil B. DeMille on a huge circular set built to represent the Coliseum in Rome. (As I have been in the Coliseum in Rome I can vouch that it was a good reproduction.)

At the time I was watching, gladiators were dueling, red paint daubed on them where they had supposedly been wounded. DeMille was up on his large camera boom roaring away with his megaphone, yelling at one actor; "Who told ya that you could act?"

DeMille was tough but good at his work. While I stood there, bemused, I was surrounded by a bevy of beautiful young women waiting to go on camera. Garlands of flowers adorned their heads and they were wearing the finest of sheer colored gowns. I made my way off the set in some embarrassment!

The administration building was half a block long and three stories high. The accounting department was located on the second floor. One evening after most of the accounting department had left, I too was on my way out. The building suddenly dropped straight down. I headed for the nearest elevator but it would not open. I joined the crowd dashing to the stairs. The stairs were jammed with writers and actors rushing down from the third and second floors. The entire building seemed to drop a foot straight down then it started to weave.

When we reached the outside we sat on benches usually used by "extra" people waiting to the called to take a part when needed. I was sitting next to W.C. Fields, the bulb-nosed comedian. True to form, he tried to turn the situation into a funny one, making one joke after another.

Paramount had been shooting a circus picture on a large sound stage opposite us. The huge end doors opened and out poured a large variety of wild animals followed by their trainers cracking whips. We watched apprehensively, none too sure that the trainers could control the lions, tigers, elephants, zebras and other wild animals, which were unexpectedly loosed from the confines of the sound stage. Though the animals were highly nervous due to the quake, the trainers managed to herd them into their carrying vans.

The shakes kept on throughout the night. As I walked home to the apartment I shared with my sister, the sidewalk started weaving up and down. I wondered if I would make it home. The shakes continued all night long. In the city of Long Beach there some four hundred people dead, and millions of dollars in property damage. Louise and I shared our experiences. She had been caught in the Colliers Magazine Building where she worked but was able to get home, finally, by street car.

Back in 1929 when on the staff of PriceWaterhouse, I noticed that Stanford and California graduates were kept on the permanent staff while others were laid off after the busy season (from October through March) was over. I determined to better my education. While working at Paramount, I enrolled in the four year course at University of California, specializing in Accounting I and II, Auditing and Business Law.

At the same time I was doing accounting at Paramount, I played in a fifty piece orchestra at Angelus Temple when Aimee McPherson was Pastor. We practiced once weekly and played Sunday mornings and evenings. Playing in the orchestra was very rewarding. When the red light went on we knew that our music was being heard over hundreds of miles from Los Angeles. Angelus Temple owned its own studios, KFSG, at the temple, and all broadcasting was Christian. Our orchestra boasted an Italian director, Berlotti, one of the finest, until Mrs. McPherson (ever dramatizing her services) wanted to put the orchestra in uniform and Berlotti resigned in protest.

I attended one year at their night Bible School, L.I.F.E. (Lighthouse of International Foursquare Evangelism). I took classes in exegesis, biblical history, and Christian writing. It was at this time that I wrote my four tracts. I prayed the Holy Spirit would guide me as I wrote the tracts. The tracts were named: Stark Blind, Hetaire, Judgment, and Your Brother.

I was amazed to find later when studying the Bible that the three tracts covered the Biblical verse "When the Holy Spirit is come He will reprove the world of righteousness, of sin and of judgment." The third tract was the admonition to go out and save your brother.

At the end of the last (fourth year) at college I was getting only five to six hours sleep a night and I became a physical wreck. I had lost twenty-five pounds and began to fall asleep in class at the university. I was glad when graduation was over.

I was so tired at the end of the four years that I went to Mr. Legace, the office Manager at Paramount, and offered my resignation, to take effect immediately. Mr. Legace tried to talk me out of it but when he finally saw I meant to leave he said, "Well, Ray, you're the boss." When going for a check up at this time a doctor said that I was either blessed or cursed with too much energy and that I had to take a rest. I took a two year furlough and travelled up and down the state just recuperating. Luckily, Paramount had covered me with an excellent health policy so I had plenty of travelling money.

I became acquainted with an English surgeon, Dr. Henry Malley, and his family. One daughter, Ruby, had curly black hair, large brown eyes, and a sunny disposition. She, too, was a student at L.I.F.E. and went on to become an evangelist. When Ruby was younger she had been offered a position in the movie studios to become a child actress but her family, being very religious, refused for her.

I remember one evening Ruby wanted to go out to Paramount Studios and tour the lot. At that time it was not customary to admit sight seeing people to the lot, but I told her I would take her in. The studios all had large steel gates with a policeman on duty. I had my ID card for my own admittance but nothing for her. The guard, however, took one look at the beautiful girl and he couldn't tell but what, from her appearance, she might have been working on a night assignment, so we were waved in.

One of the most important accounting assignments I ever had was with General Motors Acceptance Corporation. At the end of the busy certified accounting session at Price-Waterhouse, when I was on their staff in San Francisco, they suggested that I take over the setting up of the budgetary control system for General Motors Acceptance Corporation in San Francisco. This consisted of some thirteen General Motors Dealers sending in their monthly financial statements to the PriceWaterhouse office. I would then go over their financials and set up budgets for each dealership for the coming month.

Ray at Paramount Studios, age 25

All of these dealers were in the multi-million dollar classification. The financial responsibility for setting up their budgets from the operating statements was of high importance to General Motors Acceptance. They were flooring the dealer's car inventories, which amounted to millions of dollars. A profitable dealership had to be maintained under very strict controls. With my experience in every phase of the business (General Motors Headquarters in Detroit, Willys-Overland in Toledo and Detroit, as well as out in the field with Ford, Buick, Dodge, and Pontiac) I was able to render the services they needed.

General Motors Accounting system and their follow up on the dealers was second to none. This experience has been very valuable to me in my own enterprises, as it let me know what I could and could not do safely.

The last two companies I audited in San Francisco were a bus manufacturing concern that was in financial difficulties, and a large paving company. After the busy season was over I went to Lybrand, Ross Brothers and Montgomery as a Public Accountant in San Francisco. After some time with them I was offered some of their fringe accounts for auditing on my own. It was here that I started my own public accounting business in San Francisco. I picked up the bus manufacturing company and the Lowrie Paving Company, then on my own I found other accounts including the Tanner Welding Company, an independent garage.

Married Life

It was 1929, the year that the most far reaching event of my life occurred. I was attending as a loner the First Baptist Church in San Francisco. It wasn't long before a beautiful and vivacious girl, Edith Brookover, made friends with me via the flirtatious route. She told me later that she did so because she was mad at the young man who had brought her to church. As I was a willing victim of her womanly wiles I did not object to being friends and soon we were "going steady." She was in her fourth year at San Francisco State College.

She had financed her way through college by working in homes for board and room and $5.00 a month (ending at $20.00 per month plus board and room). She had won a small scholarship while at high school with grades that placed her at the top of the list. She was valedictorian for her high school graduating class. Her subject was "The Keys to a Successful Life." I was interested in her choice of subject for her speech. Some years prior I had written and published a small book entitled "True Success".

Edith was in her fourth year at old San Francisco State College, studying to become a school teacher. Her graduating class in 1937 was issued the last permanent teaching credentials ever issued by California. After that year the law was changed.

We met in October, were engaged in November, and were married on January 24th, 1937. We started married life in a two room apartment in a large apartment house across from San Francisco College when it was located downtown across from the San Francisco Mint. Being married proved more expensive than I had thought! I determined to raise my fees in my accounting business. That was a mistake, as my biggest account was the paving company with 150 men on the payroll. The owner was a rich man living in Hillsborough, down the peninsula from San Francisco. He was also Scotch and refused to pay the new fee as he could put on a permanent accountant for what I was asking for three hours work a day.

I had to move fast as I did not have any surplus to play around with. I had bought my wife an emerald wedding ring on time, (how did I know that they were more expensive than diamonds of a similar size? Besides the stone was a very choice one!) I had a Buick automobile I was buying on contract so I got busy frantically trying to increase my income. I noticed an ad in the paper by Eatmore Ice Cream (later, Meadow-Gold) for an office-credit manager in Los Gatos, California, a small town some fifty miles down the peninsula. I interviewed for the position and was hired.

I went to Los Gatos to work and Edith stayed in San Francisco to finish her last five months of college before graduating. She wanted to quit and join me but I insisted that she finish. Life is uncertain and I wanted her to be able to support herself in a decent way in case something happened to me. She says that she still hates to hear a train whistle. She commuted down to Los Gatos and back to San Francisco every weekend and that meant being separated another week. We were very much in love, no make believe about it.

I worked for Eatmore Ice Cream for five years, eventually becoming Assistant Secretary of the company as well as retaining my Office Manager's job and that of Credit Manager. They told me that I had proved to be the best Credit Manager they had ever had.

At this time I became a member of Kiwanis (I was a member for 17 years). I was a member of a golfing foursome with Paul Curtis, President of First National Bank; Dick Swanson, Vice President of Meadow-Gold; and Harry Boone, the owner of a local barber shop. We played once a week for two years until La Rinconada became a private club with membership fees in the thousands per year.

We joined the local Baptist Church where I served as Superintendent of the Sunday School for a period, then was made Secretary and after that became Treasurer. It was a small church of about three hundred members.

First Baptist Church of Los Gatos had been established for forty years and had had the same pastor for all those years. The pastor had become very dictatorial, so twenty-five of us couples decided to start another church. I was given the job of presenting to the congregation the statement of separation. My heart was not in it but I took on the job. We started our new church, which we named "Calvary Baptist Church," in a basement. The church grew. We bought four acres of land and put up some small buildings on it. Then the big building went up for a congregation of eight hundred. By 1980 Calvary Church had another beautiful building of stone, seating some 1800 people. It all started with 25 couples dedicated to the Lord's work. Calvary Church sends and supports many missionary families in many countries around the world.

Our family by this time had grown. Charleen (who later changed her name to Sheri) was born November 1937, and Glen came seventeen months later, March 16, 1939. We were poor people and our pleasures were simple. An auto drive to Santa Cruz to be on the beach was quite a thrill. In the evenings I would play my saxophones for the family. I had a favorite song for each person in the family.

Charleen Louise (Sheri)

Glen David Robertson

My favorite song for Edith was "I Love You Truly," "Mighty Like a Rose" for Glen, and "That Red-Head Gal" for Sheri. The kids would recognize their songs and would look up and grin at even a fragment of their tune idly whistled.

Five years after we had been married I started doing some private income tax work at home. One of the companies I had was the Polly Prim Bakery of Los Gatos. The Los Gatos bakery had been established thirty years and was making good money. Mr. Jacobsen, the owner, had opened a second store across the mountains in Santa Cruz.

In the meantime in December of 1941 we had built a new home on Englewood Avenue on a half acre lot we had bought at a bargain.

When I went to work for Eatmore I was promised a raise in three months but month after month went by and no raise. One day Mr. Nielsen was leaving for the San Francisco store and said, "Is there anything you want to see me about before I go?"

I said, "Yes, there is. Three months ago you promised me a raise of $25.00 a month. Here I am walking around with the seat of my pants out and I need my raise!"

"OK, Ray," Mr. Nielsen said, "You'll get your raise."

Meadow Gold sold wholesale to retail stores all over Northern California. Mr. Nielson sent me to the San Francisco retail store and also to the Oakland retail store to look over their books. The home office of Meadow Gold in Omaha had sent their auditing crew out to make an audit of our ice cream factory and its retail branches in California. They came to an auditing problem they couldn't seem to solve so they called me in on it. I worked out the answer. And it was then that Meadow Gold wanted me to join their auditing staff and go all the way to Florida for the next audit. By this time, though, I was immersed in the furnishing of our new home and had a family I did not want to leave.

Besides, I was tired of moving from audit to audit with no permanent place to call home. We liked Los Gatos, a beautiful little town nestled in the foothills of the Santa Cruz Mountains. It was close to San Jose and to San Francisco, and only twenty miles from the beach at Santa Cruz.

The President, Vice-President and I shared a large office together. Meadow Gold was building a water tower at Salinas and also another one at Paso Robles. Mr. Nielsen failed to notify me of the tower being built at Paso Robles. As a result I let building costs of the Paso Robles tower go direct to the Salinas project.

Mr. Nielsen got good and mad about the error and things were pretty uncomfortable for a while. I resented being down-graded in front of others by Mr. Neilsen's remarks. I told him I was worth $10,000.00 per year and he was paying me a mere $4000.00. That did it! He demoted me from the office manager's office and brought in his brother-in-law to be office manager, keeping me on as credit manager and assistant secretary of the company. It was an intolerable situation and I looked for a way out.

I mortgaged my home for $10,000.00 to a friend of mine, a Mr. Robert Spotswood, who regularly financed me over the years. I then resigned from the ice cream company and bought the Polly Prim Bakery directly across the street from the ice cream factory.

Polly Prim Bakery, Los Gatos, CA

We made a living in the bakery but not much more. It was heavy physical work for an office man and the hours were long. I had two bakers and myself plus some four sales girls in the store working various shifts. I did the books at night after working my shift as a cake baker. The physical work may have helped to prolong my life, however, as I am now 80 years old and still going.

Life in a bakery can be dangerous. There is always the hazard of getting a hand or the corner of an apron caught in a big mixer. I let teachers bring their classes through to tour but it was a nerve-wrecking time because I knew of a child who was scalped when her hair got caught in a mixer. The powerful biscuit cutters could give a person nightmares, too, and the oven was a menace.

When the fire box at the back of the old brick oven exploded it would knock me down. Accumulated fumes caused the explosion when I went to light the oil burning pilot. Four times the fire department came rushing down the back alley to put out the fire at Polly Prim.

Finally we borrowed money again and took out the old brick oil-fired oven and replaced it with a new eight shelf revolving electric oven that was ten feet high, twenty feet long and twenty feet wide. It was a beautiful piece of equipment costing six thousand dollars. We put down a new maple floor, bought a new steam box, and two retarding boxes to hold our finished products before baking. All equipment was of stainless steel and white enamel. Our refrigerated store cases were of walnut with glass fronts.

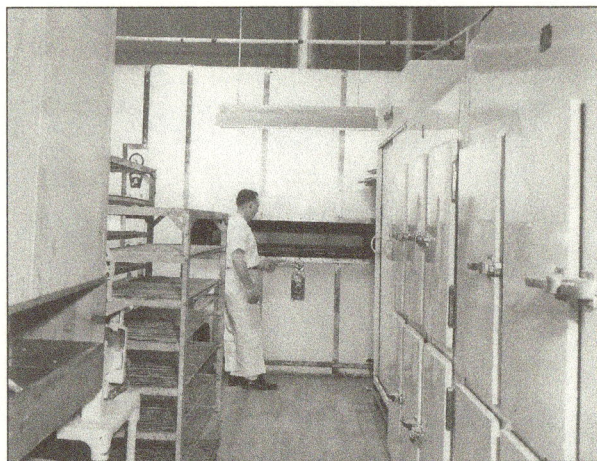

After I replaced the old oven the fire chief told me he had been on the verge of citing me for the hazard to the town. We had a good warehouse in the back for our raw materials, shortening, flour, sugar, nuts, etc. We had only one accident during the bakery years after we put in the new equipment. An electrical short developed in the operating panel. The floor around the bakery was wet at the time and when

I pushed the 220 volt button to start the oven it shorted out, gave me an awful jolt and burned a gold ring off my hand. This was nothing, however, to the four oil explosions we had with the old oil oven.

Some days things went completely wrong. I often worked feverishly to meet deadlines. One day when I was to supply the Los Gatos History Club women with twelve lemon cream pies, time was running out on me. The secretary rang, asking why the pies weren't delivered yet. They weren't delivered because they were still in the oven, but of course I told them the pies would be there shortly. Once again the phone rang, someone telling me that the ladies had finished their salads.

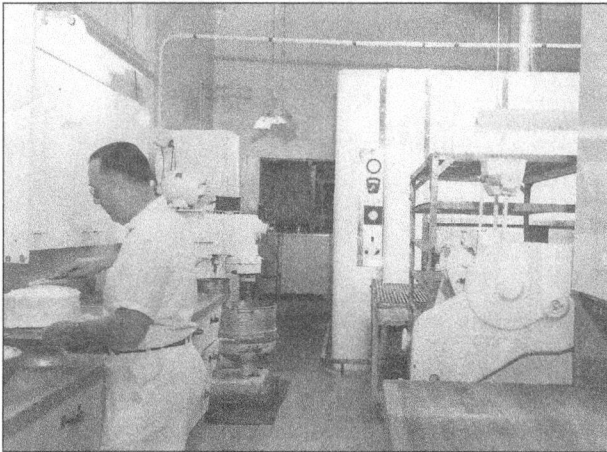

I assured them the pies would be there in time, ran to the oven to take out the first big tray with six hot lemon pies, turned quickly, caught my apron on the edge of the oven door. Down went the hot pies, splattered all over the floor. I turned, walked out through the warehouse and out to the alley.

When I recovered, I came back into the bakery, fixed up two trays of cream puffs to substitute. A salesman standing by asked me how I had managed to stay so calm. Little did he know how near a complete collapse I was.

Life became very filled. Edith was occupied with the children but I got in on some of the activities. I remember once standing at the bathroom basin shaving, my face covered with lather, little Sheri watching in amazement. "Can I lick the whipped cream off for you?" she wanted to know.

One evening as Edith and I sat reading there was too much noise in a room of supposedly sleeping children. When I growled, "What's going on in there?" ever quick-witted Glen replied, "Oh, it's just the sheets squeaking."

When Sheri was a third grader she had scarlet fever, followed by kidney infection with nephritis. She was in bed for nine weeks. Having had pneumonia when a baby, she was somewhat vulnerable. When she was a fourth grader she climbed a huge oak at Los Gatos High School, fell, and broke her arm.

Sheri took violin at school when she reached the fourth grade. She also took piano lessons, played very well. She had perfect pitch, could accomplish as much in ten minutes practice as most kids in a half hour. Glen learned to play the violin but he used his own system of reading the music. I took both kids to the San Jose Civic Auditorium to hear Spivolowsky. They greatly enjoyed the program.

Glen and I were very close, as close as we could be, that is, when I was working such long hours. When he was a small boy he used to follow me, attempted to help with all my activities. In May of 1945 Edith snapped a picture of the two of us, shirtless, bending over, raking in the back yard. When we got the picture we noticed my right breast was too large to be normal. Edith was alarmed, insisted on a doctor visit.

I had injured my right breast in the bakery. Carcinoma developed. I was hospitalized the day after my check with the doctor and the malignant growth was removed. Two weeks of x-ray treatments followed. It was thirty-seven years later I found the lymph glands were affected. When we were visiting Ruth and Kenny in Oregon I got an insect bite; the arm and hand swelled alarmingly, the arm completely filling out my shirt sleeve. After doctor treatment the swelling went down somewhat but the arm has stayed larger that natural. Later in Hawaii I injured my hand and the same swelling followed. The hospital people explained the lymph nodes were not taking out the fluids. The lymph glands still don't work well. I try to avoid all injuries to my right arm and hand.

Edith boarded kids from broken homes for a period of ten years to help with our financial problems. Her help was invaluable. We put in a swimming pool to keep the kids happy and busy.

Sheri had to have orthodontia work on her teeth, as did Happy, one of the boarders. Edith took the kids camping in the summers. I would drive over the back Santa Cruz Mountain roads to be with them on weekends. It was quite a sight to see our large tent surrounded by the kids' pup tents.

I took Glen with me to the Sierra quite a few times when we owned the tear drop trailer. I remember taking Glen to southern California with me on his first plane trip and to my surprise he read funny books all the way. The novelty of flying did not seem to faze him.

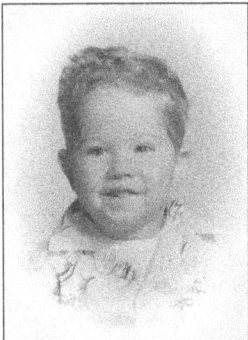

April 3, 1950 we were delighted with a new member of our family. Jon Robertson appeared on the scene and promptly had six months colic. I relieved his pain as much as possible by carrying him around and singing a little "rumpti-dump" song to him as I cuddled him against my shoulder.

Jon was a cute little kid with curly hair. With all the boarders, Happy and Terry and with his own siblings, Sheri (13) and Glen (11) he had built in baby-sitting. The kids were all so much older than Jon that he developed very rapidly. I used to tell him stories by the hour at bedtime, making them up as I went along. He never seemed to tire of my stories. He would crowd toward the wall in his bed to make room for me, cuddle down in the covers, then say, "You talk. I listen."

He followed the older kids about, watching, learning, a part of the group yet having his own independent life, too. Later on I used to bring old typewriters home for him to play with. He loved to take them apart and try to fit them together.

After ten years of owning the Polly Prim Bakery the hard physical work and long hours was getting to me. I put the bakery up for sale, determined to get into some easier business. In the middle of the night I conceived an ad;

A DREAM BAKERY, IN A DREAM TOWN, IN THE STATE OF YOUR DREAMS, CALIFORNIA!

I placed the ad in a national trade bakery magazine and sold out to one of the most prominent bakers in the world, a Max Akermann of New York City. He had been head baker for King Farouk of Egypt, Queen Wilhemina of Holland and Robert Dadeen of New York City where he had twenty-five bakers under him. He had come originally to the United States because the Swiss government wanted him to represent Switzerland at the World's Fair in New York. He had won gold cups by the dozen, they covered a large table when displayed for public view. I sent him blown up views of the bakery interior. He and his wife, Trudy, flew across the country to inspect it. They bought on sight.

After selling the Polly Prim I traveled all over the state of California trying to locate another profitable business to buy. I looked at automobile agencies, as my experience was so extensive in the industry, but I did not have the capital to swing such a big deal. Finally I found the Christian Book and Bible Store in San Diego, at the corner of fifth and Broadway, right in the center of the city. I bought it and later opened up a second store on E Street that is still in operation. Of that I am proud. The Polly Prim is still operating in Los Gatos, too. So I sold good going businesses.

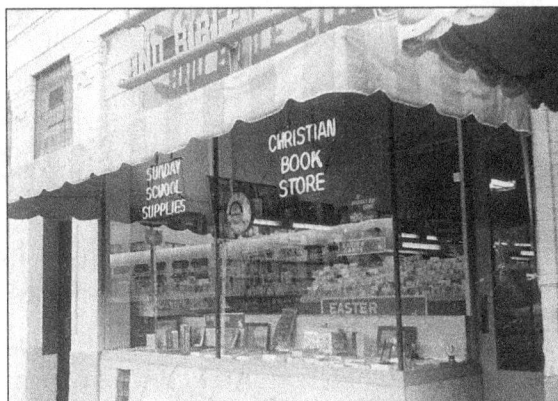

Christian Book and Bible Store in San Diego, CA.

I traveled back and forth between Los Gatos and San Diego. Jon suffered over my absences as we had a very close relationship. One day as I drove away down Englewood Avenue Jon ran away from Edith, stood in the middle of the street looking mournfully at the retreating car. Another time as I returned to San Diego Edith and Jon took me to my plane. I looked out the window to wave good-by and Jon opened his mouth in anguish, shouting, "No!"

Glen joined me during his summer vacation and began working in the book store. We rented a house in Chula Vista and Sheri came to be with us, too. Edith and Jon were left in Los Gatos to try to sell the house. The house did not sell so we rented it out. Two years later we became homesick for Los Gatos, friends, church, and our pool. We were glad we had our home to return to. Sheri, especially, was glad to get back with her friends.

I located a small Sewing Machine and Office Machines store in Los Gatos, on Main Street. Rodman, the owner, had had a heart attack. I mortgaged my home again (that being about the fourth time!) and bought the business. My heart was not in the sewing machine end of it but I did relate to the office machines. I tried to learn to demonstrate sewing machines but making buttonholes was not for me. There was too much penny-anti stuff and I could not tolerate dealing with all those women.

Business at first in the store was poor. Sam and Esther Rodman, the previous owners, had had a "closing out" sale before I bought the store and it was hard for me to get started.

The first three months I went behind $5,000.00 and I thought I had lost everything. One night I came crawling home to tell Edith I had sold nothing all day but one spool of thread! In two years, however, I outgrew the premises. We had machines piled everywhere on the floor. We had to step carefully to avoid tripping. Glen was my mainstay during those years. He worked with me, waited on trade, helped with repairs, held on for me when I took time off.

Chrislow's Department Store was moving to a new location so I rented the store they were leaving, 111 North Santa Cruz Avenue. It tripled my rent and Rodman, the prior owner, warned, "You'll never make it with that heavy rent to meet." We were in the 111 North Santa Cruz twenty-two years and our sales went up to fifteen times what they were in the little old store on Main street. In a few years we bought the building—a profitable thing to do, although it meant years of payments plus interest. All those fifteen years I kept our noses to the grindstone, kept myself on a $600.00 monthly salary in order to pay for the store. We finally paid for the building but I had not built much for my old age when I was to go on Social Security. Edith invested some $400,000.00 in our family support and into the expenses of the business through boarding children and then through her teaching.

Los Gatos Office Equipment & Supply

From two employees (just me and Glen) the store had grown to nineteen. I was very fortunate in getting my capable sister, Louise, from Los Angeles to join us. Her husband Sheldon was not well, and died a few years later, so it was good for Louise to have a secure position. Gloria, their daughter, was an outgoing teenager, soon found a host of friends. We enjoyed seeing her from time to time, always full of fun.

Louise took take charge of the bookkeeping for us and was an all-around person.

The Los Gatos Office Equipment & Supply, Inc. was at one time the number one store in the United States in the sale of the German Olympia Portable typewriter. I sold some

6,000 of them over a period of years and the company sent men out from headquarters in New Jersey to find our how we were doing it. The machine was so good that when I sold one where there were several children in the family I eventually sold all the kids, as each would take his own machine away to college. That was the big market I captured.

I won many prizes over the years for my selling. One I prize is a fine Citizen watch. It has thirty-three jewels, is self-winding, waterproof and shock proof. My jeweler claims it is the finest watch he has ever cleaned.

While at Quincy, Illinois, I had roamed the beautiful parks with my boyhood friend, Frederick Resch, and developed a love of the outdoors. Little did I dream that some day I would own a beautiful twenty acre park in the California Sierras. We had gone camping on our vacations ever since we were married (no money for any other kind of vacation) and often would find the parks crowded. We began to look for our own private place to vacation, finally found what we liked and could afford, a place on the east fork of Sutter Creek. The creek split the canyon, there was a beautiful five acre meadow, much wooded area and an outstanding hilltop giving a view for over fifty miles.

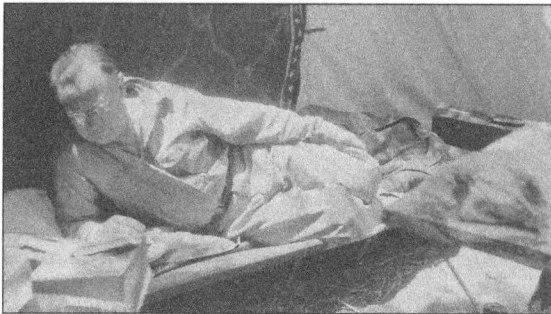

Ray at one of the early camp sites, reading of course!

We had bought a little second hand tear drop trailer in our early married years for ease in camping vacation.

Then we bought a larger trailer and took several vacation trips.

But when we found the Sierra property we bought a fifty-five foot trailer and added a twelve by fifty-five foot screened porch. It was a real home away from home.

We enjoyed going there on week ends and vacations from 1967 until in the 80's. It has been said that going for frequent recuperative periods can extend the life span some thirteen years so I may last until I am around eighty-five or ninety.

The Sierra place was a spot for family gatherings from time to time. Jon went with us during the first few years we had the trailer. Glen and Jon both got into the act of putting up fences.

Our Sheri graduated from high Los Gatos High School with highest honors, won a scholarship to College at Santa Barbara, then went on to San Jose State College, graduating with highest honors with a teaching credential. She and Miles were married before they finished college at San Jose State. They went on to Chicago, where Miles went to Moody Bible Institute to prepare for missionary work while Sheri taught fifth grade in a school in the suburbs of Chicago. After Miles graduated from Moody they moved to Denver where Sheri again taught school and Miles graduated from Denver Theological Seminary. Miles accepted a call as youth director in a church in San Bernardino. Stephen Neal Tully was their first child, born in San Bernardino. Miles joined us at Los Gatos Office Equipment when he found they could not make it financially as a youth director. David Wayne Tully was born in San Jose. I am proud of the two grandsons.

Glen, our older son, graduated from Los Gatos High School with highest honors. He went to San Jose State College for a year. He felt a call to go into Christian work, went to Moody Bible Institute in Chicago, graduating with highest honors. Then he went on to Wheaton University, graduating again with highest honors. He, by that time decided he did not want to go into Christian work but decided to become a psychologist, so went back to San Jose State, again graduated with highest honors. Glen had worked during all his high school and college vacations at the store. Glen joined the staff of Rehabilitation Mental Health Services, is now second in command. Glen and Sue were married, produced two lovely daughters, Erica Lynn and Karin Sue. Sue does important work in Santa Clara County Juvenile Department.

Our younger son, Jon, grew up with old machines around for him to play with but he entered the business world to earn a salary when he went down to the store on Saturdays and helped straighten up shelves. He has been with me in the business ever since those early shelf straightening days. When I had my heart attack he took over the physical operations as Vice-President and Manager.

There were many happy family hours together as we met for swimming at our pool or visited the Sierra property. Steve and Dave had the advantage of living in the trailer home with Sheri and Don for a year and no doubt will look back on that year at the ranch with fond memories. Holidays often brought the entire clan together. The grandkids grew up with close ties for one another.

Edith and I made a tour of Europe which included stops in Norway, Sweden, Holland, Denmark, France, England, Scotland, Switzerland, Italy and Germany. I was impressed by the cleanliness, particularly in northern Europe. The dikes of Holland were interesting to me, the way the Hollanders reclaimed so much land from the sea. In crossing the North Sea we got a taste of what we had read about. It was indeed rough, so much so that many stayed in their cabins.

In Sweden I was conscious of the many high rise apartments in Stockholm. Some apartment buildings were self-contained, had stores of every kind, even schools. No wonder the suicide rate was so high there, that life is so unnatural. We took the northern route to Norway, ended at the edge of a fiord just 300 miles from the Arctic Circle. The grandeur of the surroundings was breath taking. We got our first look at the reindeer here. In a Norwegian museum we saw Viking boats that were used in the 1200's. They had been preserved in the mud of a harbour all those centuries. We saw one of the oldest churches, made all of wood, dating to around the 1200's.

In Germany as we took a trip down the Rhine River we saw the ruins of innumerable old castles on either skyline. Boat traffic was heavy, many interesting ships with colorful cargoes passed us. We went to the Olympia factory at Wilhelmshaven on the North Sea, were given the red carpet treatment by Olympia officials who met us by limousine, gave us a tour of the factory. Edith spoke of seeing a wonderful lemon squeezer in Bremen and they sent the chauffeur to get her a half dozen! The factory showed German efficiency at its best. Overhead conveyors carried frames to be assembled, huge presses were stamping out parts. It was a great help to me in my efforts at our store to be able to tell the public how thorough the German nation is in its production methods.

I admired Switzerland. The stores were interesting and the merchandise was of real quality. Candies, cookies, cakes were unusual and watches and jewelry were of fine quality. We saw no shoddy merchandise in Switzerland or Germany.

We flew over the Alps to Italy. Here I thought the merchandise and food did not compare to that in Germany and Switzerland but I found the people delightful as contrasted with the reserved Germans and Swiss. Edith and I were lost in Rome one day on our way to meet our group for dinner.

Edith in marble - Pompei — Circa A.D. 79

A well dressed Italian lady saw our confusion and, even though she was in spike heels, insisted on accompanying us six blocks to our destination. Her courtesy was typical. We took in the Coliseum; went to Castle Grandolfo to hear the Pope address the people in four languages, blessing articles held up by the audience. I held up a Gold Cross Pen for the blessing. My Roman Catholic employee, Nat Muraco, was touched to receive the pen when we returned. We visited the underground catacombs and saw skeletons of Christians who had died there.

We flew to Lebanon, saw the Cedars of Lebanon (wood from the cedars of Lebanon was used in Solomon's temple). We caught on to the way to do business with the people of Lebanon by haggling over the article to buy. We were lucky to visit there before the war started. The hotel where we stayed was later bombed.

On another trip overseas we took in the changing of the guard at Buckingham Palace, visited the church of Charles H. Spurgeon, the Prince of Preachers, where he had preached to congregations of 10,000 people. Spurgeon has been dead 100 years but his college is still turning out preachers. I was impressed by the permanent buildings in Europe, They are built to last hundreds of years.

We visited Scotland and after Edinburgh we went south to Perth in Perthshire. I regret the tour was programmed in such a way I did not have time to look up Blair Castle, the ancestral home of the Robertsons since 1269, one of the oldest and best preserved castles in Scotland.

We visited Syria, saw the tombs of Abraham and Sarah, visited Damascus. There are many people eking out a living doing hand work on metal for tourists. Their houses have flat roofs and there they grow their vegetables. Vines up over the roof help keep the houses cool.

In the Holy Land we saw Tyre and Sidon on the Lebanese coast, an old castle built by the Crusaders, the Garden of Gethsamane, Golgatha, and other places in Jerusalem of interest to Christians. In the church built over the site of the birth of Christ we watched an old man in ragged clothes push his way forward to kneel and kiss the gold star in the pavement. It was a moving thing he did. I understood his feelings of love and adoration. When we returned to America after the long twenty-four hour flight from London to San Francisco I, too, wanted to kneel down and kiss the good old American soil!

As a baker I appreciated the bread sticks
and the ancient Babylonian brick oven

We visited Wilbur, Edith's brother, on the big island of Hawaii and liked the restful life there. We built a new home there in Hawaiian Paradise Park. Our tract was only three miles from the ocean, had 1000 one acre building sites and was only seventeen miles from Hilo. It was built of cement block. Our daughter, Sheri took her two boys (and was joined briefly by the granddaughters) and spent a month decorating and furnishing the place. She had done interior decorating when she and Miles were in business in Campbell. She decorated the house in Polynesian style. Wilbur assisted us in the planning of the grounds. We lined the driveway with cocoanut palms, made many typical tropical plantings of

bananas, citrus, guavas, pineapples and flowers. The rain-
fall there is 124 inches a year. I used to enjoy hearing it on
the metal roof at night.

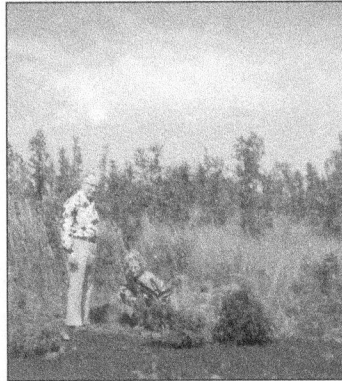

Ray & Edith at Paradise Park, HI. 1978

I found the humidity in the islands was a definite draw-
back to me as I had been used to California's dry climate. I
sold the property, being very fortunate to get almost what it
was worth.

At this writing all four grandchildren are in college. It
is my hope to live long enough to see them all graduate from
college and take up the career of their choice. I hope they be
guided into the line of endeavor in which they are happy and
are fulfilling the mission in life for which they are best suited.
Making a success in life, physically, mentally, financially and
spiritually takes real effort. My desire is that all out loved
children and grandchildren will achieve real success in these

four phases of life and in the sunset of their lives look back without regret on a happy and successful life.

As to my own profession and the life I have led, I do not believe it could have been more interesting and varied. I have outlived the Biblical three score and ten years by ten years, even though I have had two major operations (three for cancer, three for heart pacer placements), a broken leg (held together by a piece of steel), two egg-size cysts removed, a dislocated right shoulder, a diaphragm hernia, and a stroke in 1975 which left me partially paralyzed in my left hand. I apologize for listing my ailments, but what a marvelous machine the human body is and it is my belief that the will to fight has much to do with survival.

From two employees our store had grown to nineteen. Our copy department has some one hundred thousand dollars of equipment in it: small copiers, a huge collator Xerox 9600 copier and a Kodak 150 collating copier. I am President, Edith acts as Secretary, Sheri has pitched in from time to time to help when she could spare time from her own varied career. Glen is Treasurer and Jon is Vice President and General Manager.

We are assisted at the store by bookkeeper who use NCR bookkeeping machines. They handle 750 customer accounts and give us recaps at the end of the month. I (with Edith's help) take care of the financial and accounting department in the home office. We receive a report of the business made each day. The paper work is enormous. We have postage meters, calculators, copiers, bookkeeping machines, a word processor and two typewriters to aid us. We furnish the state and federal governments with nine income tax statements per year. A part time bookkeeper comes a few hours a day to help here in the executive office. It is here that all my years of experience, plus my college education, assists me.

Over the years Jon has taken hold of things downtown. He has had many innovative ideas.

105 N. Santa Cruz Ave., Los Gatos, CA

The copy department was Jon's brainchild, has been very profitable. He put in computers, has tried to keep the business growing with the times. Jon trained in computers, attended classes in Santa Clara, San Francisco and Boston. He installs computers and is a trouble shooter. He sells on the floor, manages the employees, does many hours of planning and conferencing to keep things going. It was mainly as a result of Jon's vision for bigger and better things that we made the three-way trade a few years ago that resulted in our acquiring the larger building and parking lot at 105 North Santa Cruz Avenue. Jon led in the design and planning of the new store.

Edith has been a great helpmeet for me, working year in and year out, boarding children, teaching school, then working in the home office with me. I operate as if "It really all depends on you," but I know in the end it all depends on God.

From the first week of our marriage Edith and I have followed verse ten in Malachi in the Bible which says: "Bring ye all the tithes into the storehouse, that there may be meat in my house, and prove me now, herewith, saith the Lord of hosts, if I will not open you the windows of heaven and pour you out a blessing, that there shall not be room enough to receive it."

We have never failed the Lord in respect to tithing though we did not have any idea that God would bless us so much. We're not always successful, of course but we try to follow God's word in all we do. We help several organizations with our tithe. I am trying painfully to say (and that not is boasting) is that we follow what the Lord says in every phase of our lives as near as we can, not because of what He will do for us but what we can do for Him in His command to carry the Christian gospel to the ends of the earth and to love our fellow man as ourselves.

We know we're only a heartbeat away from standing before God. It behooves us to read the Bible, follow His words, attend His church, live the Christian life to the best of our ability.

It will not be easy to be a Christian. Christ said, "In this world you shall have tribulation, but be of good cheer. I have overcome the world." I know that we who have accepted Christ as Savior will live eternally with Him as He said before He died on the cross "I go to prepare a place for you that where I am there you may be also." He also gave a word of encouragement, "Eye hath not seen nor ear heard the wonders that are prepared for you."

My life story could not be complete without this testimony as to what means the most to me in this life and in the life to come. Christianity is the hope of the world — for God so loved the world that He gave His only begotten Son to die for the sins of all the people of the world — that they might have eternal life by believing on Him as their personal Savior.

Final note by Edith:
Ray died February 4, 1987
His faith never faltered.

www.ingramcontent.com/pod-product-compliance
Lightning Source LLC
Chambersburg PA
CBHW031329040426
42443CB00005B/266